Policy Development for Special Educational Needs: A Secondary School Approach

by

Mike Gordon and Hazel Smith

A NASEN PUBLICATION

Published in 1995

© Mike Gordon and Hazel Smith

All rights reserved. No part of this publication may be reproduced or transmitted in any form or by any means, electronic, mechanical, photocopying, recording, or otherwise without the prior permission of the publishers.

ISBN 0 906730 72 4

The right of the Authors to be identified as authors of this work has been asserted by them in accordance with the Copyright, Designs and Patents Act 1988.

NASEN

Published by NASEN Enterprises Ltd.
NASEN Enterprises is a company limited by guarantee, registered in England and Wales. Company No. 2637438.

Further copies of this book and details of NASEN's many other publications may be obtained from the Publications Department at its registered office: 2, Lichfield Road, Stafford, ST17 4JX. (Tel: 01785 46872; Fax: 01785 41187)

Cover design by Graphic Images.
Typeset in Times and printed in the United Kingdom by Impress Printers (Stoke-on-Trent) Limited.

Policy Development for Special Educational Needs: A Secondary School Approach

Contents

	Page
Introduction	5
Responsibilities	7
Principles	8
Action Plan	9
From Policy to Practice	10
Content	13
The Presentation of the Policy	20
In-Service Training	21
The SEN Co-ordinator	23
Appendix A - Evaluating Integration in your School	25
Appendix B - An Example of One School's 4Ps Framework	30
References and Further Reading	32

Acknowledgements

The authors and publishers wish to express their grateful thanks to:

- the headteacher and staff of Scalby School, Scarborough, North Yorkshire, for permission to reproduce the chart in Appendix B;

- to John Elliot and the publishers of *Bridges* for permission to reproduce part of his article, first published in Vol. 1, No. 1, 1994, in Appendix A;

- to HMSO for permission to quote from Paragraph 2.10 (Page 8) of *Code of Practice on the Identification and Assessment of Special Educational Needs* (1994) which is Crown Copyright. Crown Copyright is reproduced with permission of the Controller of HMSO.

Introduction

Many members of staff in schools are understandably concerned that they will find it difficult to 'have regard to' the detailed requirements of the *Code of Practice* (1994) on the identification and assessment of special educational needs. Wide ranging duties are placed on Special Educational Needs Co-ordinators (SENCos). Support departments and existing staffing resources may not be seen to adequate to fulfil these.

This book aims to give guidance to schools and governing bodies by:

- clarifying statutory responsibilities and requirements;
- setting out the principles of good SEN policy development;
- describing practical strategies for developing, implementing and maintaining SEN policies.

The *Code* accepts that it would be unrealistic to expect all schools to have had in place, by 1 September 1994, procedures matching those in the guidance. Before initiating change schools should consider four principles of good practice:

- Remembering the uniqueness of each school, a thorough ***evaluation*** of present policy and practice should precede developmental action.
- Development of new policy and practice to meet the requirements of the *Code* should be ***gradual*** and based on planned and realistic targets.
- A policy is never finalised but is ***dynamic*** and subject to continual improvement.
- Policy development is not the task of one person or a working group but involves the active participation of the governing body and the ***whole school staff***.

The educational context

All education, not just that part of it which is devoted to special educational needs, has been subject to unprecedented change over recent years. The 1980s saw many national initiatives, for example, TVEI, LAPP and National Curriculum arrangements. Concomitantly, throughout the decade there was a gradual shift of power away from Local Education Authorities to central government or to individual institutions and local authority management structures were substantially reorganised.

The *Education Act,* 1988, has had a radical effect on the context in which planners and providers for special educational needs operate. This Act did not have pupils with special educational needs as a main priority and many of its requirements do not sit easily with the principles underlying the *Education Act,* 1981. The increasing devolution of financial management from LEAs to schools, plus a policy of open enrolment, has placed schools in direct competition with each other in order to maintain their pupil numbers. In these circumstances pupils with special needs may not be offered high priority and many authorities have found it more difficult to plan coherent services for them.

The Audit Commission and HMI (1992) were critical of SEN providers in their operation of the *Education Act,* 1981, and advocated changes in practice within the framework of the *Education Act,* 1988. The *Education (Schools) Act,* 1992, introduced new arrangements for inspection to be carried out by OFSTED (Office for Standards in Education) and these are described in Technical Paper 8 (*OFSTED Handbook for the Inspection of Schools,* May, 1994).

The *Education Act,* 1981, placed statutory requirements on schools towards all pupils with special educational needs, including duties:

- to use their best endeavours on behalf of all such pupils; and

- to integrate those pupils in the work of the school as a whole.

In addition, the *Education Act,* 1993, requires school governing bodies to:

- publish information on their SEN policies by 1 August 1995;

- report annually on the implementation and success of those policies in the first annual report published after that date, and in all subsequent reports;

- summarise their SEN policies in the prospectuses which they publish, as from the autumn of 1995;

- have regard to the *Code of Practice* as from 1 September 1994.

Having regard to the *Code of Practice* means that, in deciding how they will organise support to children with special educational needs, schools must consider the guidance in the *Code* and then ensure that school policy and practice measure up to it.

Whilst acknowledging that recent legislation and requirements present many challenges to schools this can also be seen as a time of opportunity. In particular, the requirements of the *Code of Practice* should lead to an enhanced status for work in the SEN area and increased awareness and professional development for all staff.

Responsibilities

The governing body
The *overall statutory responsibility* for determining the school's general policy and approach to provision for children with special educational needs lies with the governing body. Clearly this should have the central role in setting policy aims, in their implementation and in overseeing the policy-making process. However, there should be recognition that school staff will have the expertise to undertake the detailed policy development work and, in some cases, it may be more appropriate and realistic for them to take the lead.

The headteacher
The governing body will need to work closely with the headteacher who will be responsible for the *day-to-day management* of all aspects of the school's work, including special educational provision, and who will keep the governing body fully informed. In practice, responsibility for this management is likely to be assumed by the SENCo.

The Special Educational Needs Co-ordinator (SENCo)
The headteacher will work closely with the SENCo or team, who will have *day-to-day operation* of the school's SEN policy.

The school staff
All the staff, both teaching and non-teaching, should be *involved in the development* of the policy, be fully aware of the school's SEN procedures and be clear about their responsibilities in the implementation of the policy.

Principles

The SEN policy should clearly describe the school's intended educational practice and this should inform the action of all staff. It should contain specific targets and information on how performance will be evaluated.

Policy targets should be realistic and achievable. It will be necessary to take into consideration:

- existing SEN practice within the school;

- the resources available within the school and provided by the local authority;

- the current organisation and physical structure of the school;

- the skills, experience and attitudes of the staff;

- the expectations of the pupils, parents and local community;

- the local authority's SEN policy and audit system.

It will be essential for schools to continually review and evaluate provision. The following set of principles may provide a useful reference point:

- Equality of provision should be the basis for work to meet special educational needs.

- All pupils with special educational needs should have full access to all appropriate provision including the National Curriculum and this should be relevant and differentiated.

- Support for pupils with special educational needs should be given in the least restrictive environment and, wherever possible, within the ordinary classroom setting.

- Opportunities for all forms of integration with those who do not have special educational needs should be maximised.

- Assessment and provision should be made in partnership and collaboration with those who have special educational needs, their parents and carers.

- Provision should be staged and flexible to reflect the variety of the continuum of need.

- All staff have a shared responsibility to provide for pupils with special educational needs.

- A high standard of special needs provision will only be possible if there are appropriate opportunities for curriculum and professional development for all staff involved.

Action Plan

Governing bodies and schools will establish their own procedures for SEN policy development. The following is a possible course of action:

The school's governing body

Schools will have had experience in drawing up policies on a range of issues and will be able to build on this when planning procedures for SEN policy development. The governors will need to appoint a member to be responsible for SEN coordination. For large schools it may be advisable to set up a special educational needs committee and perhaps sub-committees with distinctive briefs, such as for curriculum and finance. The governing body will need to prescribe clearly the purpose and work of those with designated responsibilities.

The governors have responsibility for determining who shall have the duties of policy development. In consultation with the headteacher, and the SENCo, the governors will decide the composition, remit and timetable for the working group. The working group should include representatives from faculties or subject areas who could liaise between the SENCo and their own departments as the policy is developed.

The involvement of all staff and the feeling of ownership which this produces means that the process of developing the policy may be regarded as of equal, or even greater importance, than the final document.

The working group

At its first meeting, the group will decide on its procedures and begin a programme of work which includes:

- considering the requirements of the *Code* and possible additions and amendments to existing policy. Deciding on priorities and drawing up a new draft policy (see the following section, **From Policy to Practice**, and Section 5, **Content**);

- consulting with interested parties including senior management, governors, departments, non-teaching staff and parents;

- working with pastoral and specialist staff to incorporate or take into account existing policies for pupils with emotional and behavioural difficulties;

- identifying professional development needs and planning whole school in-service training on the requirements of the *Code of Practice* as appropriate;

- modifying the policy in the light of consultation;

- reporting to the governing body which will then discuss and ratify the policy contents if they are agreed.

The policy document is then published and distributed or made available to appropriate people. The policy is used as a framework for practice which will require on-going monitoring and evaluation within the school. External policy appraisal will be provided by the local education authority and OFSTED.

From Policy To Practice

When all the basic information specified in the regulations is included the policy document may be rather lengthy. Schools may wish to produce a prefatory or separate statement which is concise and summarises the SEN policy. This should show a clear link between the values and beliefs of the school and its practice.

The framework proposed by Facherty, Howes and Turner (1992) and further developed by Palmer, Redfearn and Smith (1994) is particularly useful for developing special educational needs policies and is based on the **Four P's of Policy**.

Philosophy

Statements of the school's beliefs and values are the starting points for developing policy. They set out where the school is starting from. An example is, 'Parents should be involved as partners in the education of their children'.

Principles

After stating the school's beliefs the intentions for putting these into practice are given. For example, 'Parents' knowledge and views should be utilised as fully as possible in assessing and meeting the special educational needs of their children'.

Procedures

This section specifies the practical steps that will be taken to achieve what the school is setting out to do. For example, 'Parents will be kept informed about progress and action and their views will be sought on a termly basis'.

Performance

Statements in this section will describe how the implementation of the policy will be evaluated. It will indicate how quantifiable evidence can be collected and presented to demonstrate the effectiveness of the school's SEN provision. For example, 'Records of parental contributions and attendance at reviews'.

When the statements for the 4 Ps are combined there should be a clear and accessible picture of the school's SEN priorities and what it is trying to do. Some statements, in particular those following the statements of philosophy, will be modified or withdrawn in subsequent years as the school continually refines its policy and practice and achieves targets.

Appendix B - gives an example of one school's use of the 4 Ps framework.

The *Code of Practice* specifies the information to be included in the school's SEN policy:

1. Basic information about the school's special educational provision:
   - the objectives of the school's SEN policy
   - the name of the school's SEN coordinator or teacher responsible for the day-to-day operation of the SEN policy
   - the arrangements for coordinating educational provision for pupils with SEN
   - admission arrangements
   - any SEN specialism and any special units
   - any special facilities which increase or assist access to the school by pupils with SEN

2. Information about the school's policies for identification, assessment and provision for all pupils with SEN:
   - the allocation of resources to and amongst pupils with SEN
   - identification and assessment arrangements; and review procedures
   - arrangements for providing access for pupils with SEN to a balanced and broadly based curriculum, including the National Curriculum
   - how children with special educational needs are integrated within the school as a whole
   - criteria for evaluating the success of the school's SEN policy
   - arrangements for considering complaints about special educational provision within the school

3. Information about the school's staffing policies and partnership with bodies beyond the schools:
   - the school's arrangements for SEN in-service training
   - use made of teachers and facilities from outside the school, including support services
   - arrangements for partnership with parents
   - links with other mainstream schools and special schools, including arrangements when pupils change schools or leave school
   - links with health and social services, educational welfare services and any voluntary organisations.

Education (Special Educational Needs) (Information) Regulations, regulation 2 and Schedule 1.

Figure 1: The School's SEN policy (taken from the Code of Practice, 1994, Paragraph 2:10).

Content

There is no requirement to follow a set format in setting out the school's policy. However, it is probably useful to consider the areas that need to be covered in the order in which they appear in the *Code of Practice,* (see *Figure 1*). More detail relating to the relevant information can be found in *The Organisation of Special Educational Provision,* DFE Circular, 6.94.

Basic Information

What are the objectives of the SEN Policy?

Within this section should be set out the principles which underly the school's arrangements for SEN provision for both statemented and non-statemented pupils. Objectives will need to be determined. The arrangements outlined in the SEN policy will seek to secure them. These should be in a form which is easily understood and can be evaluated as part of the requirement of the annual report. *The Four P's of Policy (Appendix B)* considers the setting of objectives in greater detail.

Who is the SEN Co-ordinator?

Arrangements for organisation of SEN provision will vary from school to school, and it may be useful at this point to name other staff, for example any member of senior management with an overview of SEN, or staff with responsibility for provision within a specialist unit.

What are the arrangements for co-ordinating educational provision for pupils with SEN?

As more detailed information is required regarding assessment and teaching arrangements in Section 2 of the policy outline, a broad outline will suffice at this point. It could be linked to the role of the co-ordinator and include reference to the arrangements made for:

- oversight and updating of records for pupils with SEN;
- advice to and liaison with subject colleagues;
- input to departmental meetings;
- 'link' staff from departments;
- SENCo involvement at Stages 2 and 3;
- input to curriculum development.

What are the school's admission arrangements?

Reference to admission arrangements is made in paragraphs 34 and 35 of *Circular 6.94* which affirm that the policy for pupils with SEN but without a statement will have been considered in the light of the school's general admission arrangements. It also states that:

> 'Whilst LEAs and schools can make any reasonable and objective admission arrangements in the event of over-subscription, those arrangements cannot be used to refuse admission to a child - or give the child lower priority than other applicants - simply because the school considers that it cannot cater for his or her special educational needs' (Para. 34).

Information is also required if admission arrangements give priority to pupils with SEN, for example in schools where there are special adaptations for pupils with disabilities:

> 'The SEN policy should also specify whether the school or LEA gives priority in admitting children who could make use of the facilities, including access arrangements. The number of places allocated under special criteria for educational reasons should not exceed ten per cent of the total intake' (Para. 35).

Has the school any SEN specialism or special unit?

If the school has specialist unit, for example for pupils with visual or hearing impairment or for those with moderate learning difficulties, the policy should give information relating to this. This will need to include details of the staffing, specialist facilities and equipment, and arrangements made for supporting pupils within the unit and integrating them within the school as a whole.

Are there special facilities which assist access to the school for pupils with SEN?

If the school has any special adaptations or expertise which increase ease of access they should be described. These might include lifts and ramps, adapted cloakroom and lavatories and lighting or colour coding which aids visually impaired pupils. The policy could also mention further adaptations which are planned or needed.

Information about the school's policies for identification, assessment and provision for all pupils with SEN

How are resources allocated to and among pupils with SEN?

The information included in this section will vary considerably according to the local authority, and many SENCos writing their policy might find this a difficult area to address. Considerable confusion exists in many areas regarding exactly how much of the school budget is designated for special needs, especially for non-statemented pupils. The formula for funding may be based on proxy indicators such as the number of pupils receiving free school meals and there may be allowances for social priority areas, service pupils and ethnic minorities. The situation is further complicated by the variations in the levels of delegated funding to schools in different LEAs, some having total delegation of funds for statemented and non-statemented pupils and others holding the funding centrally.

If the amount targeted on SEN can be identified, probably with the assistance of the school's LMS officer, then discussion will need to take place with senior management in order to explain exactly its distribution, bearing in mind that this will need to be included in the Governors' Report. Reference will need to be made to the staffing of the SEN department and how staff are deployed, whether in teaching classes, sets, or small groups, or supporting pupils in subject classes. It may also be necessary to refer to class sizes in general, particularly where pupils are 'set' or 'banded', as the benefits of a reduced group size are frequently given as part of the provision for pupils with SEN. Additionally, it should be pointed out that special educational needs occur across the whole ability range.

What are the school's identification, assessment and review procedures?

Identification of pupils with SEN will usually begin even before pupils enter Year 7 and reference will need to be made to the liaison procedures at primary/secondary transfer. These could include details of:

- visits by SEN and pastoral staff to primary schools to meet pupils and staff;

- visits by pupils to the receiving school;

- parental visits and interviews;

- National Curriculum assessment evidence;

- details of previous SEN arrangements, including Stage level and IEPs, (Individual Education Plans);

- reports from primary or feeder schools and external support services.

Standardised tests may be used to screen the new intake and the policy should give details of these and of any further diagnostic procedures which provide additional information relating to pupils for whom the screening test results give cause for concern. The policy will also need to indicate the strategies used to place pupils on the SEN Register at the appropriate stage. In some authorities standardised procedures with accompanying criteria may be in place, but in others schools may need to draw up their own criteria and documentation with reference to paragraphs 2:61 to 2:98 of the *Code* for the school-based Stages 1 and 2, and 2:99 to 2:120 for Stage 3 where outside agencies are involved.

Details of identification of pupils at Stages 1 and 2 will need to make reference to arrangements made across subject departments to identify pupils at these stages.

Paragraph 2:73 of the *Code* states:

'The child's teacher or tutor will gather information about the child and make an initial assessment of the child's special educational needs'.

Obviously, in a secondary school, although the form tutor may be involved in collating the information, he or she cannot be responsible for assessing the pupil's needs across the complete curriculum. Schools may need to consider carefully the most effective and efficient method of fulfiling this requirement depending upon the pastoral/tutoring structure of the school and the time available to the SEN co-ordinator for administration.

Identification and assessment at Stage 3 will need to include criteria for referral to outside agencies such as support services and the procedures which follow such referral. Most local authorities will have given guidance to schools on these.

In outlining review procedures, details of arrangements within school to review pupils will be needed, and of the timing of such reviews. Review procedures will need to include reference to progress made within subject areas. This might be as part of an end of topic or module assessment or by completion of a form circulated by the form tutor at Stage 1 or the SENCo at Stages 2 and 3. The reviewing process will also need to include communicating with both parents and pupils regarding progress made by the pupil and future arrangements. The policy should outline how this will be carried out, whether by official review meetings, parents evenings, or informal contact with the parent by the form of year tutor or SENCo.

What are the arrangements for providing access to the curriculum?

All pupils are entitled to a balanced and broadly based curriculum, including the National Curriculum. The arrangements for access to this may include reference to any banding or setting within subjects, and any areas of the curriculum where in-class support and withdrawal teaching might be provided. If the full range of subjects is not available to all pupils, then details of restrictions, disapplications and alternative provision should be given.

Reference should also be made to departmental policies where details of differentiation for pupils with SEN within a subject area may be found, and to the drawing up of IEPs for pupils at Stage 2 and above.

How are pupils with special needs integrated within the school?

Paragraphs 45 to 47 of **Circular 6.94** outline the need for pupils with special educational needs to join in the range of school activities. Reference is made to break and lunchtime and to the use of support staff at these times. Mention is also made of school visits and social activities. If the school has special arrangements in place to support pupil in any of these areas they should be described. If such arrangements to ensure equal opportunity are not in place, are they appropriate and do they need to be considered?

John Elliot (1994) has produced a useful framework of questions which any school evaluation of integration should address. This is included in *Appendix A*.

What are the criteria for evaluating the success of the policy?

In its policy the school will need to set out how it proposes to demonstrate the effective implementation of the policy and may have indicated specific targets against which the success of particular aspects can be measured.

The success of the policy in the light of these targets can then be included in the annual report to parents.

What arrangements are in place for considering complaints about SEN provision in school?

Hopefully, any difficulties regarding SEN provision in school can be resolved amicably and informally. The first point of contact in such situations will probably be the child's form tutor or the SEN Co-ordinator. If the matter needs to be taken further, then it may pass to a deputy headteacher, or whichever member of the senior management has an overview of SEN, and then finally to the headteacher or governing body. If the matter is unresolved at this level, then the LEA complaints procedure will need to be followed and details of this should be included in the policy. Reference should also be made to the LEA arrangements for SEN Tribunals for appeals against LEA decisions relating to statutory assessment.

Information about the school's staffing policies and partnership with bodies beyond the school
What are the school's arrangements for SEN in-service training?

This might include arrangements both for in-service outside the school for the SENCo or other members of staff, possibly leading to a particular qualification relating to SEN, or may include details of 'in-house' arrangements.

- Has there been any in-service for all staff relating to the requirements of the *Code of Practice*?

- Has the SENCo been able to provide INSET for subject departments, working with them to update their departmental policies with reference to provision for pupils with SEN?

- Is there planned INSET to address areas such as differentiation of the curriculum?

The policy may also refer to the in-service needs of non-teaching staff working with pupils with SEN and of any training for governing bodies. As the SEN in-service training policy should be part of the school's development plan, there will need to be liaison with the school's INSET co-ordinator and consideration of the INSET budget so that priorities can be established and written into the SEN policy.

What use is made of teachers and facilities outside the school, including support services?

The content of this section will vary according to the range and level of support services provided by the LEA and to the amount of delegation of funding for SEN which has taken place.

If the school has regular visits from professionals such as educational psychologists, learning and behaviour support teachers, specialist teachers for the visually or hearing impaired or education social workers/welfare officers, they can be detailed here. Information may include the frequency of visits and liaison meetings, and the names of personnel involved could be appended to the policy. If a service level agreement is in place, then details of this can be given. It will also be necessary to set out the school's criteria for referral to outside agencies and the procedures which are followed prior to this. It may be useful to include examples of any SEN record forms and of referral forms to outside agencies if these are used.

How is partnership with parents arranged?

Paragraphs 2:28 to 2:33 of the *Code of Practice* outlined in some detail possible parent partnership arrangements, and lay emphasis on the importance of parental involvement in the pupil's progress and on the unique knowledge of the child held by the parent. The policy will need to consider the methods by which the parent is made to feel confident in his or her relationship with the school, whether in formal meetings and parental interviews or in informal contact with staff. The policy should also give details of any LEA arrangements regarding Parent Partnership Officers working with parents of pupils undergoing statutory assessment, naming the officer and giving contact details.

What links exist with other mainstream and special schools, and what arrangements are in place for when pupils transfer to other schools or leave school?

Some mainstream school have established links with local special schools. These may include the attendance of pupils from the mainstream school on a part-time basis at the special school, possibly for a particular activity such as a 'corrective reading' group, or an interchange of staff, or an exchange of resources. Any of these activities which assist in the school's provision for SEN should be included here. If arrangements exist for the part-time integration of pupils from the special school within the mainstream these should also be outlined. The policy will also need to describe procedures for transfer of information between schools and of any special arrangements which are made to support pupils with SEN prior to leaving school.

How are links established with health and social services, educational welfare services and voluntary organisations?
Paragraphs 2:38 to 2:60 of the *Code of Practice* deal with health, social and educational welfare services. *The Children Act,* 1989, and the *Education Act,* 1993, lay emphasis on the importance of cooperation between schools and these services. The school will probably already have regular contact with the health services through the school doctor, but the policy could set out the processes for contacting him or her, together with procedures for informing parents.

Social Services may have an officer designated to work with pupils with SEN in schools and details of the contact procedures for this and any other agencies working with the school should be included. It may also be useful to include the names and contact address of the personnel involved.

The Presentation Of The Policy

In presenting the policy it will be necessary to consider the prospective audience when decisions are made regarding style and format. Although a professional appearance is obviously desirable, it will also need to be user-friendly. Some schools may wish to distribute copies of the policy to parents of pupils with special educational needs, but it must be readily available to all parents. A summary of the policy should be included in the school brochure.

The policy is likely to contain a great deal of practical information, but will also reflect the aims and ethos of the school. It may be decided to separate the aims and objectives of the policy from the practical and administrative sections. It may also be useful to use a loose-leaf format in order that information can be regularly updated, and to include an appendix of names and addresses of personnel outside the school who are involved with pupils with SEN, and examples of school and local authority documentation.

In-service Training

The implementation of the requirements of the *Code of Practice* will undoubtedly require some in-service training, both for Special Educational Needs co-ordinators and for staff as a whole. As has been stated earlier, while the SENCo may be responsible for the drafting of the SEN policy, all staff will need to be involved in its final form and in its effective implementation. Funding has been available to LEAs through the DFE GEST funding for training relating to SEN policies.

The authors were involved in delivering INSET to SENCos and Headteachers in both primary and secondary schools in North Yorkshire. The feedback from this initial INSET, and follow-up questionnaires to schools, indicated that secondary SENCos felt that they needed further training to meet the requirements of the *Code of Practice,* and that there was also a need for considerable INSET directed at subject teachers. Areas identified included:

For SENCos:

- SEN Policy development;
- supporting other staff;
- individual education programmes;
- assessment.

For both SENCos and subject staff:

- differentiation;
- specific learning difficulties;
- reading difficulties;
- spelling;
- handwriting problems;
- difficulties in mathematics;
- behaviour management.

Given that school budgets are limited, it may be that the SENCo will be involved in the delivery of INSET to the rest of the staff. Indeed, Paragraph 2:14 of the *Code,* in describing the responsibilities of the SENCo, lists both, 'liaising with and advising fellow teachers' and 'contributing to the in-service training of staff'. If this role does fall to the SENCo, then he or she will need to consider carefully how best to approach the task.

A possible model might involve:

1. An initial meeting with senior management and/or governors to outline the implications of the recent statutory requirements and regulations.

2. Whole-school INSET relating to the *Code,* with particular emphasis on Stages 1 and 2 where much of the responsibility for pupils with SEN is with form tutors and subject staff. However, all staff will need to be aware of procedures and responsibilities at Stages 3, 4 and 5.

3. INSET with subject departments to assist in their reviewing of their present provision for pupils with SEN, identification of areas which need to be addressed, and establishing priorities and the timescale for all this.

How the priorities established might be achieved could provide a focus for further INSET relating to curriculum delivery, which could either be with departments, via departmental meetings, or the whole school using training days or twilight sessions. It may also be useful to survey the whole staff in order to identify their perceived training needs.

Frequent reference to differentiation is made in the *Code of Practice,* and particularly to the responsibilities of the class or subject teacher at Stages 1 and 2. Many staff still feel ill-equipped to tackle this task and, as well as relevant INSET, financial support and time will be needed for resources to be developed.

A possible way forward could involve asking staff to examine their present methods of curriculum delivery, and hopefully to reassure them that they already use many differentiation techniques. This could be followed by listing areas which could provide a focus for INSET such as, readability and related text-based work, information technology (IT), the production of worksheets and materials, specific learning difficulties, and contribution to IEPs. Staff could then indicate which of these they would find most useful and relevant to their subject area. It may also be profitable to try to negotiate the timing of INSET so that it suits the maximum number of staff involved, although such flexibility is not always possible.

It is important that the SEN policy and its resourcing are viewed within the context of the overall school development plan and that the SENCo liaises closely with the school's in-service co-ordinator.

The SEN Co-ordinator

Although the responsibilities of the SENCo are outlined in paragraph 2:14 of the *Code of Practice*, they may be much more demanding and wide-ranging than this. They are likely to include:

- maintaining the school's SEN register and pupil records;

- preparing and reviewing (for the governing body) the SEN policy;

- liaising with and advising teacher colleagues;

- liaising/working with parents of pupils with SEN;

- liaising with external agencies and primary/secondary/special schools;

- contributing to the in-service training of staff;

- developing and maintaining resources for SEN;

- support teaching for children with SEN;

- identifying and assessing SEN (including monitoring and evaluation);

- preparing, or co-ordinating preparation of, individual education plans, (Stages 2 and 3);

- organising and attending review meetings.

The response to many of these responsibilities will be set out in some detail in the SEN policy, including the coordination of provision for pupils, liaison with parents and outside agencies, and contribution to staff in-service. In order for the Co-ordinator to fulfil his or her role effectively, he or she will need considerable support. Support will be provided by senior management in the school in order to establish the development of an SEN policy as a priority for all staff. This can be demonstrated by financial support and by time for related INSET both for the Co-ordinator and other staff.

The SENCo cannot be expected to deliver quality INSET to other staff or to implement the requirements of the *Code* unless he or she has had adequate training and feels confident to cope with the challenges that the *Code* presents.

Informal support can be provided by regular links with Co-ordinators where information can be shared regarding policy and practice within schools in the local area. In some LEAs, Co-ordinator meetings are established and supply cover provided. In others, the meetings are informal and take place outside the working day. Whichever is the case they can provide a vital support in what is often a very lonely job.

The LEA can also provide support by ensuring that its procedures are clearly laid down, that information is effectively and speedily distributed, and by the provision of appropriate documentation for record keeping.

APPENDIX A
Evaluating Integration In Your School

Using a series of non-hierarchical headings, this framework identifies the major issues which any school evaluation of integration should address. A limited number of related questions are offered as starters to your enquiries.

1. **The broad purpose of integration:**

    a. Does integration achieve locational integration for each child with a Statement?

    b. Does integration achieve social integration for each child with a Statement?

    c. Does integration achieve functional integration for each child with a Statement?

    d. Does integration contribute to equality of opportunity for all children?

2. **Parents and families of children with statements:**

    a. Can the school demonstrate that there is a partnership with parents? What performance indicators are being used to demonstrate effective partnership?

    b. Do all staff - teaching, classroom support, secretarial, maintenance - use positive strategies when in contact with parents, eg. telephone manner, body language, form of address?

    c. Does the school environment present as being positive and welcoming to parents, eg. entrance hall, interview/counselling room?

    d. Are parents fully informed about the school and the work it does with their child?

    What strategies are used to ensure that parents are fully informed?

    e. Are parents informed/involved in assessments/reviews?

f. Do parents know about curriculum decisions affecting their child?

g. Do parents know who is on the governing body of the school, and who is the governor with designated interest in special needs?

h. Do parents know which school staff and other professionals are currently working with their child?

i. Do parents know a key/designated person on the school staff who is their first point of contact in the school on matters related to their child?

3. **The children with officially recorded statements of special educational needs:**

    a. Are children with statements contributing to evaluation of the integration process? Are there school strategies to encourage this?

    b. Are children with statements informed/involved in assessment/reviews?

    c. Do these children know what are the objectives for their placement in the school?

    d. Do these children know what are the current academic, social/behavioural and physical skills objectives for their work in the school?

4. **School management and systems:**

    a. Does integration receive active support from the school's senior management team? What indicators are used to demonstrate support from senior management?

    b. Does the school have a written policy for integration which is 'owned' by all staff, and has strategies to implement, evaluate and modify the policy?

    c. Does each member of staff involved in integration have a specified role which is outlined in written form? Do all persons involved in integration know what these specified roles are?

d. Can the school identify strategies used to promote a team approach to integration?

   e. Does the school have specified management procedures for obtaining resources for integration?

   f. Do school management procedures include time for staff planning, liaison and evaluation of work programmes and procedures for integration?

   g. Do the school management systems include procedures to support the transition of children with officially recorded statements of special educational needs into the next phase of education, eg. primary to secondary schooling?

   h. Do school senior management and their systems ensure there is a programme of staff development and training related to integration?

   i. Does the school have a member at the appropriate management level who has the experience and training for coordinating and oversight responsibility for integration activity in the school?

5. **Staff development and training:**

   a. Does staff development and training ensure that all staff are aware of school policy, objectives and procedures on integration?

   b. Does staff development and training assist all staff to develop the knowledge and skills to understand and contribute to integration activity in the school - teachers, classroom assistants, secretaries, maintenance, lunch-time supervisors, care and medical assistants?

   c. Does staff development and training promote consultancy and liaison skills amongst the staff?

6. **Resources for integration:**

   a. What is the financial contribution of children with officially recorded statements of special needs to the school budget? How is the spending of this money prioritised? How effectively and efficiently is this money used?

b. What staffing is invested in integration - teaching and other? How is the work of this group of staff prioritised? How effectively and efficiently are these staff used?

c. What particular transport provision is involved in facilitating integration? How effectively and efficiently does this provision work?

d. What specialist aids and appliances contribute to integration? How effectively and efficiently are these aids and appliances used? How effective and efficient are the procedures for funding and obtaining these aids and appliances?

e. What specialist therapies, psychological and other support agencies contribute to integration? How effective and efficient are the procedures for obtaining and funding support from these agencies?

7. **The education programme for integration:**

   a. Is education for children with statements taking place within a broad and balanced high quality curriculum for the school/teaching group as a whole? Do indicators used by the school to monitor and evaluate the whole school education programme inform the response to this question?

   b. Are the needs of the integrated individual or small group related to the whole class needs without reducing the quality of the provision for any children?

   c. Has each child with a statement got an individualised education programme which is integrated with the curriculum of the class/school?

   d. Does recording for each child with special needs include clear information about each child's achievement in each academic subject, and skills and competencies in social/behavioural and physical development?

   e. Does the annual review for each child with an officially recorded statement provide clear information on current achievements (reflecting statutory requirements for all children), propose specific achievement objectives for the period up to the next review, and clear information about the current placement needs for the child?

8. **Individualised Education Programmes (IEP):**

   a. Does each IEP give a supportive framework for the staff team delivering the IEP?

   b. Does each member of the team delivering the elements of an IEP have a copy of the IEP for each child they are currently working with?

   c. Does each IEP give a good assessment of the child's needs?

   d. Does each IEP take account of the school context?

   e. Does each IEP have long term and a limited number of short term objectives?

   f. Does each IEP specify the contribution from individual professionals, parents and child?

   g. Does each IEP specify required resources, and who will provide these?

   h. Does each IEP inform evaluation, recording and planning?

   i. Does each IEP provide a practical basis for parent liaison and information?

   j. Does each IEP protect the rights of the individual child and facilitate equality of opportunity for children in the school?

   This framework has been taken from 'Evaluation of the Integration of Children with Special Educational Needs into Mainstream Schools in England', John Elliott, 1994, Bridges, Vol. 1, No. 1.

APPEN
One Sch[

Philosophy (The School believes that:)	Principles (The School intends that:)
Pupils with SEN are the shared responsibility of all staff.	Each Department outlines, in its policy, how it is going to meet the needs of pupils with SEN within its subject area. Subject teachers, with the help of the Special Needs Department, will have responsibility for pupils with SEN.
Pupils with SEN are entitled to a broad, balanced and relevant curriculum which is differentiated to ensure maximum progress.	Pupils are placed in small sets in subjects where setting is the norm. Subject teachers will increase differentiation within the pupils' normal classroom work. Appropriate support is given to a pupil with SEN at end of unit tests and external examinations.
There should be a flexible and staged structure of provision for meeting SEN.	All pupils will be recorded on the SEN register at the appropriate stage. Referral and documentation will be operated in line with the school's Special Needs Policy.
Pupils with SEN will require additional resourcing to meet their needs.	IEPs will be operated for pupils on stage 2-5 and support provided according to their need.
All staff should have maximum awareness of SEN and appropriate professional skills.	Staff will have the opportunity to attend in-service courses.
Pupils with SEN should be integrated as fully as possible into the educational and social life of the school and their needs met in the least restrictive environment.	All in-class support strategies will be explored as fully as possible.
Parents should be involved as partners in the education of their children.	Parents' knowledge and views should be utilised as fully as possible in assessing and meeting the special needs of their child.

Framework

Procedures (The School hopes to achieve this by:)	Performance (We shall check/evaluate by:)
Information will be passed, through the link teacher system, to all staff. All staff will be involved in the development and implementation of the SEN policy.	Staff access to the information being disseminated on individual pupils. Comments made at Departmental meetings.
Teachers will include information on differentiation in policies, termly plans and when recording progress. Pupils are supported where appropriate either in-class or by withdrawal. Close contact with the external examination boards.	Teacher's records, pupil's work, differentiated material available. Special considerations during external examinations.
The SEN Co-ordinator, in consultation with the subject teacher and the support services, will maintain an up-to-date SEN register.	Monitoring the number of children at different stages and transfer from and between stages.
The SEN Co-ordinator, with the subject teacher and appropriate member of the support services, will plan IEPs and organise additional resources. The identification of staff development needs and provision of access to courses.	The number of IEPs. Record of Support Service involvement. Levels of additional resourcing. Teacher time allocated to pupils with SEN. The number of staff attending school based and external courses.
Differentiated curricula. Support for the class teacher. Identification of interests and preferences of pupils with SEN. Pastoral guidance.	Success of pupils with SEN in external examinations. Success of pupils with SEN in end of unit tests. Level of participation of pupils with SEN in school activities
Parents kept informed about progress and action, and their views sought on a regular basis. Response to parental concern. Parents sharing in the development of their child.	Record of parental contributions. Attendance at reviews. Parental interest and involvement at home. Timed response to parental concern.

References and Further Reading

Bentley, A, Russell, P and Stubbs, P (1994) *An Agenda for Action,* National Children's Bureau: London.

Butt, N and Scott, E (1994) 'Individual Education Programmes in Secondary Schools', *Support for Learning,* Volume 9, 1.

DFE (1994) *Code of Practice on the Identification and Assessment of Special Educational Needs,* Department for Education: London.

DFE (1994) *Special Educational Needs: A Guide for Parents,* Department for Education: London.

Elliott, J A (1994) 'Evaluation of the Integration of Children with Special Educational Needs into Mainstream Schools in England', *Bridges,* Volume 1, 1.

Hull, J (1994) *Assessment and Record Sheets for Special Educational Needs in Mainstream Schools, School Based Stages 1 - 3, Record Sheet Pack,* NASEN: Stafford.

Hull, J (1994) *Assessment and Record Keeping for Special Educational Needs in Schools, Staff Development Package,* NASEN: Stafford.

OFSTED (1994) (3rd Edition) *Handbook for the Inspection of Schools,* HMSO: London.

Palmer, C, Redfearn, R and Smith, K (1994) 'The Four P's of Policy', *British Journal of Special Education,* 21.1.

Richmond, R C (1994) 'The Code of Practice in Schools: Learning from Recording of Achievement', *British Journal of Special Education,* 21.4.

Visser, J (1993) *Differentiation: Making it Work,* NASEN: Stafford.

Visser, J (Ed) (1994) *A Guide to the 1994 Code of Practice, OFSTED Inspections and Related Documents,* NASEN: Stafford.